INSTAGRAM SECRETS (VOL.2)

How to build the perfect INSTAGRAM PROFILE

Become an Influencer and build a Business with no money on Instagram

Short social media marketing book

By Rossitza Toneva

Text Copyright 2020© Rossitza Toneva

Legal & Disclaimer

The content and information in this book have been provided for educational and entertainment purposes only. The content and information contained in this book have been compiled from sources deemed reliable, and it is accurate to the best of the Author's knowledge, information, and belief. However, the author cannot guarantee its accuracy and validity and cannot be held liable for any errors or omissions. Neither is any liability assumed for damages from the use of the information contained in this book.

No patent liability is assumed concerning the use of the information contained herein.

You agree to accept all risks of using the information presented inside this book.

First edition

How can I get money with my Instagram profile?

"The best way to predict your future is to create it." Abraham Lincoln

You have in your hands the first volume of twelve pieces puzzle named "Instagram Secrets". This puzzle includes the following pieces:

HOW to find the right Instagram AUDIENCE?
HOW to Build the Perfect Instagram PROFILE?
HOW to create Instagram KILLER CONTENTS?
HOW to outsmart Instagram ALGORITHM?
HOW to use Instagram HASHTAGS?
HOW to use Instagram METRICS?
HOW to use Instagram DIRECT MESSAGING?
HOW to use Instagram IGTV content?
HOW to use Instagram CONTESTS?
HOW to use Instagram INFLUENCERS?
HOW to use Instagram AUTOMATION TOOLS?
How to generate PROFITS from Instagram?

Each element above contribute to growing your Instagram account. You have to understand the secrets of all twelve pieces. That's why I created a set of 12 books. Thanks to this step- by –step set of books, you are going to learn a lot of tricks that nobody shares with you.

Instagram is the main social media platform, with over a billion monthly users, 71% of whom are under 35. So if you want to build a business and your target is millennials, Instagram is the right communication platform.

Keep in mind that there are three major ways to make money on Instagram.

- Work as an influencer to post content sponsored by brands.
- Be an affiliate marketer selling other people's products.
- Become or be an entrepreneur and sell your products or service.

You can learn more about these specific topics in the last book of the collection: Instagram Secrets Vol 12: How to generate PROFITS from Instagram. Become an influencer and build a business with no money on Instagram.

So keep reading all twelve books.

You can find the entire books collection in the next pages:

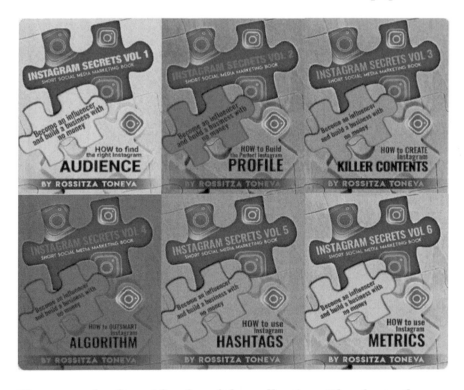

These are the first 6 books of the collection. Thanks to these first books you are going to learn the basic Instagram tools: AUDIENCE; PROFILE; KILLER CONTENTS ALGORITHM; HASHTAGS; METRICS.

The next image contains the other six books: DIRECT MESSAGING; IGTV CONTENT; CONTEST; INFLUENCERS; AUTOMATION TOOLS; PROFITS.

So once you read through, this set of 12 books I am convinced you are going to become a real Instagram expert. Make sure that you read and understand each book before you move to the next one. You will quickly see that all book strategies are connected. Only when you get the whole picture you can fully understand how to create your Winning Instagram strategy.

Think that thanks to Instagram you could turn your passions in money and build a business, but before you must know all the Powerful Secrets.

Growing your Instagram following requires consistent commitment and dedication. You will not get the results you are looking for if you are not working and build your Instagram page every single day. So you need to think about: What you are looking to get out of Instagram?

Why are you making an Instagram account?

What kind of goals you want to achieve with your Instagram account: follower growth, brand awareness or just revenue?

All my short step by step guides have a section, named Homework task. So take your time to write down your ideas. I am going to help you to clarify your ideas guiding you step by step.

Homework section is really important because it offers you the opportunity to understand what to do in this first stage of the work. Try to experiment with all the ideas that you write down in the Homework section, using your Instagram profile. When you write down your ideas you automatically focus your full attention on them. Remember that you have to experiment.

Before I start I would like to give you a special bonus - the opportunity to get one of my books for free, just sending me an email at rtineva80@gmail.com.

Please do not forget, if you enjoyed this book and found some benefit in reading it, to post a review on Amazon. Your feedback and support will help me to greatly improve my writing craft for future projects. And make this book even better.

In this specific short guide, I'll discuss in-depth tactics and strategies on how to define your own Instagram profile.

Why you should read this book?

This book is for all Instagram users that are interested in Organic Growth of their account, investing only their time. That means you don't buy fake followers, use farmed accounts to build your following, invest money in agencies or expansive campaigns. You want to attract real people who are interested in your content investing no money.

So your **Instagram BIO** is one of the first things customers and Instagram users see. Occasionally, someone may see one of your photos before they come to your profile. But if they're going to follow you, they will see your bio. So what impression are you making on them?

We all know the value of a good first impression. Instagram is no exception. So it's important to have a great Instagram bio that draws in users and encourages them to follow you.

If you want to improve your Instagram Profile BIO, here you can find some suggestions to consider.

If you have some problem with the terminology used, consult the last chapter of this book, named: "Common Instagram terms you should know"?

Introduction

What is an **Instagram BIO**? BIO is the biography of your profile on Instagram. This is your place to tell the world a little bit about yourself. An Instagram biography (BIO) is the first thing users stumble across when looking at your Instagram profile. Sometimes they might see your photos first, but your Instagram bio is what users tend to look at when deciding whether or not to follow you.

Creating an interesting and creative Instagram bio that grabs your audience's attention should be a key priority for all brands and influencers.

Most Instagram users will quickly scan through your Instagram bio and photos and swiftly decide whether or not to follow you, so you don't have long to grab their attention. Building a loyal Instagram following isn't easy—it may look like it is but, in reality, quick judgments by users can make it tough to grow.

In this book, you will understand the key elements you need to create the best Instagram profile for your brand. So, I'm going to walk you through how to create a perfect Instagram profile, and some fabulous tricks you can use to impress your followers.

Thanks to this short guide you are going to learn:

How to set up an Instagram account?

Which are the main elements of an Instagram profile?

What is an Instagram Bio?

How to create a perfect Profile that generates sales?

I am going to offer you some practical examples and homework sections that can help you to create your Perfect Profile.

Table of content

How can I get money with my Instagram profile? _____ 3

Why you should read this book? _____ 7

Introduction _____ 9

Chapter 1: How to set up an Instagram account?_____ 13

Chapter 2: What is Instagram Bio and Profile?_____ 21

Chapter 3: Tips to create a perfect Instagram profile_____ 23

Chapter 4: The Anatomy of a Perfect Profile that generate sales. _____ 39

Chapter 5: Examples of Awesome Instagram profiles. _____ 47

Chapter 6: Homework Tasks _____ 51

Conclusions _____ 55

Other books_____ 57

About the author _____ 59

One last thing _____ 63

Common Instagram terms you should know_____ 65

Chapter 1: How to set up an Instagram account?

Instagram is primarily used on a phone. You can find some steps to follow to start using this app. If you have already Instagram account skip to Chapter 2: What is Instagram BIO?

Download the app

If you've never used Instagram, start by downloading the app. Instagram is available for smartphones, tablets, and computers through the Apple iOS, Google Play, and Windows app stores.

The app is geared toward mobile devices, and you'll probably use a smartphone or tablet for most of your posting activity.

You can visit the Instagram website or use the app on a desktop computer if those options work better for you. However, some mobile features are not available or require special plug-ins to work for desktops and regular web browsers.

So, for the purposes of this guide, let's focus on using the mobile app.

Create an account

Launch the app, and create an account in one of two ways:

Option 1: Sign up with your email address or phone number, and then enter a username.

Option 2: If you have a Facebook account, you can log in with the same information and link the accounts.

Already have an account? Just sign in, and go straight to your profile page.

Register an account. Select "Register with E-mail" to sign up with your e-mail address or "Register with Facebook" to register using your Facebook account.

If you registered using your e-mail, enter a username and password and then complete your profile. Tap "Done" when finished.

If you opt to use Facebook to register, simply log in using your Facebook username and password.

Connect to Facebook.

Instagram asks for permission to manage your Facebook pages. Look through the list of Facebook business pages you've already created. Select the right page, and click "Next."

Only an admin on the account can complete this step. You won't see the page if you're just an authorized user. You can follow the following steps:

Step 1: Go to your profile and tap the "**three lines**" at the top right of your profile.

Step 2: Tap the gear icon for "Settings."

Step 3: Tap icon "Account".

Step 4: Tap icon "Linked accounts".

Step 5: Connect to "Facebook"

Turn your profile from "Personal" to "Business"

By default, you begin with a personal profile. To use Instagram for business, you have to connect your account to a Facebook business page. Click the profile icon at the bottom right of the screen.

At the top right corner of the page, open the settings menu. It appears as a vertical ellipsis in Android or a gear in iOS. You can find all step by step process below:

Tap the three (3) lines icon ($\equiv$) in the top-right corner of your profile.

1. Tap the gear icon for "Settings."
2. Next, hit "Account."
3. Then hit "Switch to Business Profile."

4. Connect to your business Facebook profile if you have one, and add additional business details as directed by Instagram.
5. Tap "Done."

Complete the profile setup

To finish your profile, enter an email, phone number, and address for your business. You have to fill in at least one of these contact fields to proceed. Some information will be auto-filled if it already appears on your Facebook page.

Click "Done," and go to your profile. A new graph icon should appear at the top of the Instagram app. This is your Insights page, where you can keep track of promotions and engagement stats.

At any time, you can go back to the profile page and switch back to a personal account.

Edit your profile

Go back to your profile page, and click "Edit your profile." Here, you can add a photo, bio, and website link. If you switched from a personal account, consider changing the photo, name, and username to reflect your business.

Using your brand's logo and business name makes it easier for customers to find you on Instagram. You can make a logo in minutes if you don't have a design yet.

Make a brief statement about what your business does or how you help customers. Keep in mind, you're free to use a more casual tone on Instagram, even if your business is conservative.

From time to time, many brands change their bio to display fun announcements on the main page.

Invite contacts to follow you

Take advantage of any work you've done to build contacts online. In Instagram Settings Menu, tap "Follow and Invite Friends" use the "Invite Facebook friends" option to send a notification to your entire Facebook network.

You can use the "Invite friends" option to access other networks, such as Gmail, LinkedIn, Twitter, or Yahoo! contacts. The more followers you have, the more it gives your business social media credibility.

Fill your gallery

Start adding photos to your gallery.

The best thing about Instagram is your ability to reinvent old photos by adding filters.

Users love the authenticity of the platform, so you don't need pro skills to tell great stories.

Click the cross-shaped "Add +" button to open a gallery from your phone. You can select the drop-down arrow at the top of the screen to get photos from other sources, such as Google Drive.

Once you know how to use Instagram, you can create Stories to drive engagement. Instagram stories are short photo or video collections that disappear after 24 hours. This simple feature is an effective way to share a funny, educational or heartwarming moment with your followers.

Even better, you have unlimited ways to be creative with storytelling. Instagram may seem intimidating at first, but the short, visual posts make it easy to learn fast and connect frequently with little effort.

Creating multiple accounts

The last point to discuss is how many Instagram accounts can handle one device?

Instagram allows you to manage up to five accounts. But you'll need separate emails for each one. So you can easily manage multiple Instagram Accounts just with Account Switching. If you've already created multiple Instagram accounts, you can simply connect them, so skip to the next section. Here's how to create a new Instagram account that will instantly be connected to your current one.

To add multiple Instagram accounts:
- Go to your profile and Tap the three (3) lines icon ($\equiv$) in the top-right corner of your profile.
- Tap the gear icon at the bottom for Settings.

- Tap Account.
- Scroll down and tap Add Account. It's near the bottom.
- Tap "Log into Existing Account". Enter the username and password of the account you'd like to add. Or log .in with Facebook if that's how you set up the other account.

Why you have to handle two Instagram accounts? If you want to have one for business and one for fun. Maintaining separate accounts is highly recommended. DO NOT use the same email or phone for your second Instagram account.

You MUST have different emails or phone numbers to recover your account!

And, per Instagram, if you sign up with email, make sure you enter your email address correctly and choose an email address that only you can access. If you log out and forget your password, you'll need to be able to access your email to get back into your Instagram account.

Chapter 2: What is Instagram Bio and Profile?

On your Instagram profile, your bio sits underneath your name and company name, making it the perfect place to share critical information about yourself and your brand.

It might have a description of who you are and what you do, as well as a snappy and enticing summary of your brand, more generally, such as what you're selling and what your brand does.

Your **Instagram BIO** is the first thing that potential followers, other influencers, and future brand partners see when they visit your profile.

See the picture below to understand where the BIO area is located.

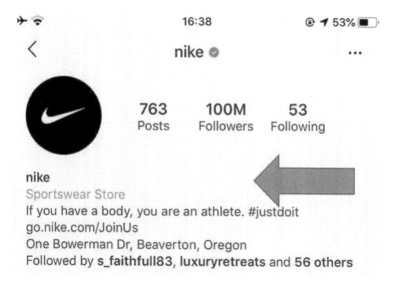

BIO makes part of the Instagram profile. Instagram Profile is composed of five elements.

Username: Nike
Name: Sportswear Store
Bio: If you have a body, you are an athlete #justdoit
One Bowerman Dr, Beaverton, Oregon
Clickable link: Nike.com
Picture: Profile picture
Thanks to the next chapter we are going to learn some tips on how to create a perfect Instagram profile.

Chapter 3: Tips to create a perfect Instagram profile.

If you want to grow your audience and attract new business opportunities, here are some do's and don'ts when updating Your IG profile.

In this chapter, you will learn how to create:
- Instagram Username
- Instagram Name
- Instagram Picture
- Instagram Bio
- Instagram Clickable link

INSTAGRAM USERNAME

This is the name that you register with, and the most important as it reflects what your account is about. Although you can change your name at any time, it is recommended that you choose one name and stick with it.

Username forms your Instagram profile URL (http://instgram.com/username) and gives your profile page its brand name.

My URL and username is
http://instgram.com/Rosyontravel.
USERNAME: ROSYONTRAVEL

Always consider does the username reflects what or who I am trying to represent?

Think about Vol 1 book: Instagram Secrets Vol 1: **HOW to find the right Instagram AUDIENCE.**

Do you remember that the most important thing is to define very well your Target market and Target Audience?

Say your Target Audience is people that love to travel. And you are an account posting about travel, then you need to make sure to include a travel or similar name in the username. For example, my account is for travel so my name is RosyOnTravel.

This may seem incredibly obvious, but there are so many people who use names that do not reflect what their account is about or what it is meant to represent.

The reason why this is so important is that Instagram is able to recognize and categorize content: nature, luxury, humor (e.g. memes), etc.

Instagram is also able to recognize which type of content is being posted on accounts. If your name does not match the content being posted, why would people want to follow it? They wouldn't.

Instead of leaving this decision to the user, Instagram will simply not show your account on the Explore feed as often because your account will have a lower viewer-retention rate.

Finding the perfect username

For accounts with a clear offering or theme, follow this step-by-step guide to determine your perfect username.
1. Write down 20 keywords that come to your mind regarding your theme.
2. Make combinations of all 20 keywords and try them out as the username.
This way you are capturing the largest possible audience as these words represent your theme. When people think of your theme and your content, they will connect with these words. This will greatly up your chances of being seen by your target audience.
As you can see, the username is "travel". My username handle should relate to what I am going to post. Don't give Instagram a reason to reduce your reach after posting your very first picture.
3. Consider only name easy to write/pronounce/understand. This is the user experience side of the Instagram search. If you have a name that is easy to pronounce and remember more people will search for your account.
If you were given the choice to search for @rosyontravel or @rosy_on_travel, which one would you be more likely to search for? Obviously the first, which means it will rank higher in Instagram search.
Here it's important to put yourself in the average users' shoes and ask yourself, "What would increase my likelihood of searching for an account on Instagram?" A memorable and easily-spelled name is a large part of increasing viewer-retention.

INSTAGRAM NAME

If you click on Edit Profile, the first field you will find is Name. The Name field, in fact, makes up the first 30 characters of your Instagram profile and is key to helping with Instagram SEO. (SEO stands for Search Engine Optimization, and it describes the logic behind the ranking of your profile when you perform a search on a particular search engine (such as Instagram or Google). In short, SEO can be defined as a digital marketing strategy that helps increase the quantity and quality of the traffic to your Instagram profile.

Essentially, there are three Profile key elements: Account Name; Account Username and Picture. And that's why these three elements are very important. The image below illustrates how Instagram searches works and what you see when you tap "Travel" in your search bar.

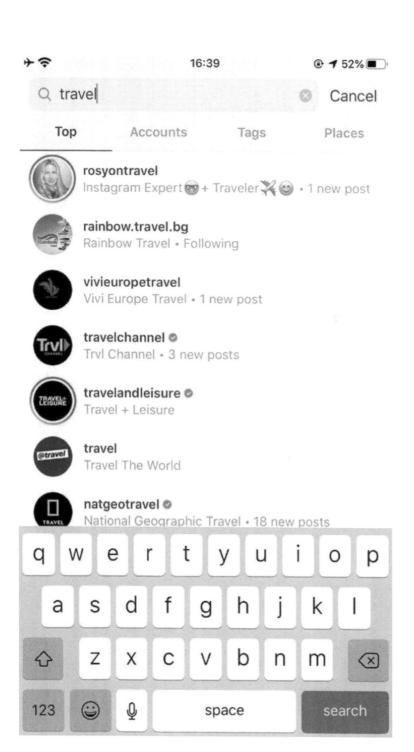

As you understood my Instagram name is the following:

Instagram Expert 🌐 + Traveler ✈️ ☺️

Here you can find some tips to use when you create your Instagram name.

Use keywords

When people search on Instagram, the words in the Name field are analyzed for matches. So if you want to rank well in searches from an Instagram SEO perspective, it is crucial you use keywords relevant to your niche in the Name section (not necessarily your business name, as the title suggests).
That's the name under your profile picture, and it's the second key element in winning at Instagram search.
It allows you to further position your account in a certain niche and increase visibility for users. Here it is important to describe your account or what you do in the shortest way possible. When people search for words in the search bar, Instagram will pick up what is written in your Name section.
Again, put yourself in your target audience's shoes. What would they search for if they are looking for your account?
Consider: what do I want to tell my followers and how can I do this in the shortest way possible?
You don't have a lot of space so get straight to the point.
A simple first step is to search for the most popular hashtags in your niche.
Note that I added emojis in my Name section because people search for these as well.
Take a look at the numbers:
Instagram: 418 million times
Expert: 1 million times
Traveler: 38.8 million times
Emojis
"airplane": 1.3 million times

Smile": 4.8 million times

These all add up to maximum visibility on Instagram.

Apply this formula to rise to the top of Instagram search is fundamental.

By applying these simple tips, anyone can maximize their Instagram SEO.

Use Emojis

Using emojis in your Instagram bio will give your profile a visually fresh and fun feel while helping your brand stand out from the crowd.

Emojis also take up less space than words, enabling you to add extra info about your brand that the character count wouldn't allow for with text.

Here are some top tips for using emojis in your Instagram bio:

•Be creative and try a combination of words interspersed with emojis.

•Use emojis to emphasize key points in your content, or as bullet points to break up the text and make it easier to read.

•Emojis should always be relevant to your brand and add value to your bio.

It is not a good idea to use just emojis on their own with no text. This can be confusing to your audience and is a waste of precious brand promotion space.

And remember, once chosen, emojis aren't set in stone. Play around with different emojis over time to see what fits best with your brand.

How to check the visibility of one emoji or word on Instagram?

1. Enter in your Instagram.
2. Tap search lens.
3. Insert an emoji as "smile" or word as example below and tap the "Tags" section.

4. You can find that Instagram has 4.8M posts with "smile" emoji.

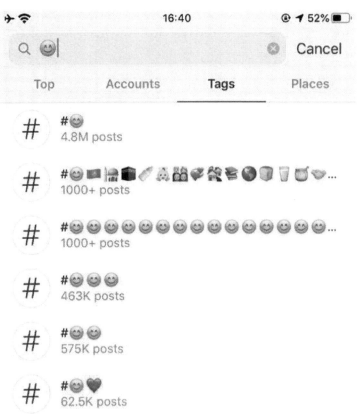

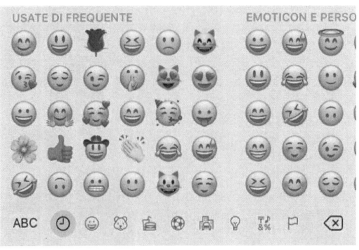

In 2020, though, emojis are too big of a cultural force to ignore. They're present in every form of digital communication, from email to Instagram to WhatsApp. In fact, did you know that 92% of all internet users now use emojis?

Your brand can jump on the popularity and influence of emojis on social media to make your message stand out, entertain your followers, and come across as more human and relatable.

Think about it, on Facebook Messenger alone, over 900M emojis are sent every day without text.

INSTAGRAM PICTURE

You don't necessarily have to use a professional camera to come up professional-looking photo. There are phones now that allow you to capture and edit photos that are Instagram-perfect. The quality of images you use in your posts plays a considerable part in Instagram marketing, as it will determine whether a person will follow you or not. You can find some tips below.

Show your face

Put a personal face on your business – unless you're a known brand, or your business is widely recognized by your logo, use your face as your Profile Photo. People don't "connect" with a logo – they connect with a face. People actually tend to ignore logos but are hard-wired to pay attention to faces. These businesses should show their face:

- Coach or consultant.
- Solopreneur or freelancer.
- One-on-one service providers.
- Influencers (or influencer wannabes).

Build the know-like-trust factor on social media by using a headshot, not a logo.

A profile picture mistake I often see is showing too much of the body, which makes the face quite small. In the photo stream, your Instagram Profile photo is tiny. Crop to head and a bit of shoulder.

It's not about your hair and clothing, it's about your face — that's what will draw people in, and help them recognize you as they see you time and again!

Resist the temptation to show something "cute" as your avatar, especially if it doesn't relate to your brand. Your face is your best calling card.

Make sure your photo is crisp and clear, and you look professional.

Choose a neutral background

A neutral or muted background works best. Keep it simple — you don't want a bunch of clutter in the background competing for attention.

Find a soft light source

Your best bet is near a window, or in open shade outside (that means bright shade). Then, face the light!

Remember that clothes make the brand

While we won't be showing much of your outfit, do wear something near your face that fits your brand aesthetic.
Adventurers, dress for adventure.
Public speakers and corporate consultants should dress like they're ready to take the stage or speak to the CEO.

Smile and show some personality!

Remember that people do business with people they know, like, and trust. The first step to being likable is to smile. Make eye contact, and show your personality in your pose! Positive vibes attract. Neutral expressions are boring.

Think about Instagram profile Picture Size

The Instagram DP size is a mere 152 pixels in diameter on desktop. On a phone, it's a scanty 110. I recommend you start with a larger image! A 500-pixel square will work on any social network. You can upload any size image, and scale and crop as you wish.

How to add or change profile picture?

You can also add a profile picture or change your current one when viewing Instagram on the web. To add, delete, or change your profile picture:
Step 1: Tap "Edit profile"
Step 2: Tap "Change Profile Photo".

Step 3: Choose to upload a new photo or remove your current one. You can choose one of your pictures from the Library "Choose from Library".

I have created a book where I'll teach you how to come up with great-looking photos that will immediately draw people's attention, consult: **Instagram Secrets Vol 3: HOW to CREATE Instagram KILLER CONTENTS, Become an influencer and build a business with no money on Instagram.**

INSTAGRAM BIO

An Instagram bio has to make an impact on your audience. It has to tell people what your business is, what you do, and why they need you. It also has to convince people to not only follow you but to also complete a particular task of your choosing (like visiting your website).

Your bio will be one of the first things users will see once they come across your account. The tricky part about writing your bio is that it's limited to a **hundred and fifty words**. That means every word you include in your bio description counts. It's a good thing that you can place a hashtag in your bio, and you can take advantage of that, too. Think of your bio as your business slogan. Make it concise yet vibrant and actionable. Through your bio, let your audience know who you are, what you do, and what you can offer that has the potential to change their lives.

And as you are only allowed 150 characters for your bio (plus the 30 characters for your Instagram Name) this is not an easy task! So let's have a look at what text you should include in your bio.

Specific niche or service
– If you are in a specific profession or industry niche, or are known for offering a particular service, then it is important to make this clear in your Instagram bio to help you immediately connect with the right crowd.

Skills and Experience
– Sharing your skills and experience will help present a professional business, building trust with your target audience and giving them an insight into what you offer.

Hobbies and interests – If your brand is based on you as an individual, then building a relationship with your followers is key. Share a bit about who you are – your hobbies, interests, values, and beliefs – to come across as likable and engaging.

Use hashtags - Adding your branded hashtag to your bio is another important Instagram strategy. This will help not only drive post engagement but also create a community around your brand. (For example, I have created my branded hashtag named: rosyontravel)

By giving your followers a way to share their content with you and your community via your branded hashtag, you will quickly create a strong interactive hub on Instagram.

Call to action - Your Instagram bio is the perfect place to add a call to action. Tell your audience what you want them to do, and if possible, how to do it.

For example, ask your audience to follow you on Instagram or other social media channels. If your organization provides a service, display your email to encourage people to get in touch for a discussion or quote.

Brick-and-mortar stores should include their address and opening times so people can easily find and visit them.

If you want your audience to open a particular web page, ask them to do so and then add the URL to the Website field.

Instagram allows you to space out your bio vertically. This set up is easy to achieve through your Phone Note app. Note app can help you to organize better your BIO text.

INSTAGRAM CLICKABLE LINK

The only place where a clickable link is allowed within the Instagram platform is the box in your bio that says, 'website,' and you'd want to take advantage of that. But don't just add a link there and leave it altogether. A good trick would be to change the link now and then depending on how often you publish new content. You can actually update the URL if you want to point your followers to new content, such as a blog page, a YouTube video, or a product page.

Now, the challenging part is to get followers to click that link since it's hidden in your bio page and not visible on your posts. One way you can get followers to click that link is to refer to it in captions you add to new posts. For instance, if you're posting a new photo, you can include something in the caption that says, "Check out the link in bio." Again, you can edit the link in your bio anytime you want.

Consider linking to your latest product page, a landing page for a recent marketing campaign, your newest blog content, or the contact page.

There are many possibilities here, so make the most of the link in your Instagram bio by changing it up in line with your business objectives.

However, your Instagram bio doesn't need to be static—shake it up a bit. Try out different emojis, calls to action, text, and more.

By varying your IG bio, you will find out what your audience responds to and what works for your business.

Chapter 4: The Anatomy of a Perfect Profile that generate sales.

It takes a few tenths of a second for an Instagram user to form an opinion about your brand online. This is why you must know how to make an excellent first impression with your Instagram business profile. Here are a few things you need to get right to give potential customers a reason to follow you and engage with your business.

Keep Your Profile Public

No one lights a lamp and then covers it with a jar or hides it under a bed, right? For your profile to be seen by the whole world (yes, you want the entire world and not just a few people to know that you exist), make sure that your profile is in public. Instagram actually keeps it that way by default, and you wouldn't want it to be otherwise. By keeping your profile public, anyone in the world will be able to view your posts, comment on your posts, and follow your account if they want.

On the contrary, if you choose to set your profile on private, only those who are already connecting to you will be able to see your posts and follow you. The rest of the world won't be able to view your photos and videos and follow you. To make sure your profile is set to "public," open the Options by clicking the three dots if you're using Android or the gear button if you're using iOs, and check whether "Private Account" is turned off or not.

You have to do the following steps: Settings – Privacy – Account Privacy and then turn on "Public". You have to see the following as illustrated below.

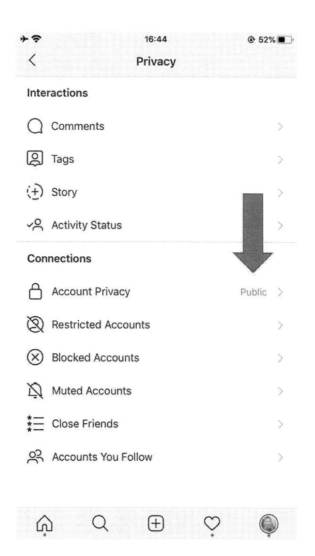

Use a Recognizable Handle and Business Name

Your handle or username should be the same as your business name as much as possible. There are cases when your business name may already be taken. If that's the case, make sure you keep your business name as part of your username, preferably the first part.

This will increase the chances of followers to come across your profile if they search for you online. In the same manner, you want to make sure that your business name is easily searchable. You can do that by adding the full name of your business to your profile's "name" section. This will appear right below your Instagram handle. You can change this by going to "Edit Profile" and clicking on the space to the right of the clipboard icon.

Examples: Starbucks and Nike Instagram profile

Use a Similar Profile Picture That You Use On Other Social Networks

If there's one thing people will see first when they come across your Instagram profile, it's your profile photo.

It's prominently displayed at the top right corner of your page, so it's impossible to miss. For that reason, your profile photo should be something that your followers would easily recognize. As much as possible, it should be the same photo you use on other marketing materials you have online or offline.

Also, keep in mind that Instagram crops your profile picture into a circle; exactly 110 pixels (on the phone) in diameter once you upload it to the site. There's no need to crop your photo into a circle yourself. Ideally, you'd want to upload a square photo with your company logo at the dead center, making sure the corners won't be excluded once Instagram has done the cropping.

Make it easy for followers to get in touch with you.

Insert your email address or website in order to facilitate direct contact with you. Another thing you should consider including in your bio is some important information in regards to your business. Whether you work with other people or simply own your personal blog, it is a good idea to include a link to your website as well as your business email.

It would be best to leave out any more private information such as your personal email as you could always come across people that could take advantage of your will to be open with your followers.

Additionally, you can also include your business's working hours and the phone number your potential customers will be able to call for more information. All of these details will help add more credibility to your brand and make your business seem more reliable and professional.

Use a call-to-action.

If you're looking for a fun way to interact with anyone new that comes across your page, a call-to-action phrase could help you achieve just that. Call-to-action phrases are sentences that motivate the reader to share something about them or act on your call to action.
A simple example can be used with the help of your aforementioned, personalized hashtag. You can simply urge your new followers to share a picture on their profiles using your hashtag. This will help bring more attention to your profile and get your audience to participate more.

Choose a unique font.

In case you didn't know, you can use different fonts for your Instagram bio without an issue. While these are not provided by the platform, they can easily be found through various mobile apps and also online websites. These special fonts help bring a fun twist to your bio and can help you showcase your character. You can use websites such as LingoJam's Font Changer and the FontFix app for your mobile device and enjoy creating and choosing from a variety of font.

Chapter 5: Examples of Awesome Instagram profiles.

You can find some examples below:

Branded BIO: AirBnB

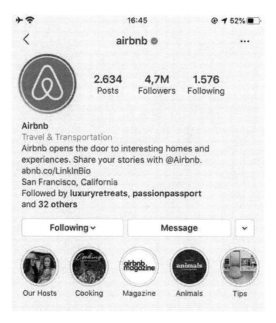

Name: Travel & Transportation
Username: Airbnb
BIO: Airbnb opens the door to interesting homes and experiences. Share your stories with @Airbnb San Francisco, California
Clickable link: abnb.co/LinklnBio
Call to action: Share your stories with @Airbnb

Public Figure BIO: KIM KARDASHIAN

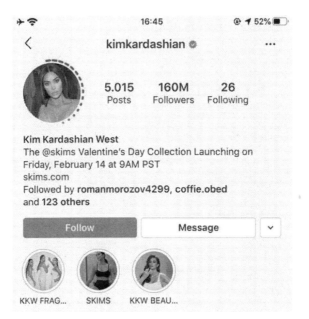

Name: Kim Kardashian West
Username: KimKardashian
Bio: Shop the new @kkwbeauty Glitz & Glam collection exclusively on KKWBEAUTY.COM and the new @skims Cozy and Sleep Collection on SKIMS.COM
Clickable link: smarturi.it/playKKHGame

My personal BIO: RosyOnTravel

Name: Instagram Expert + Traveler ☺
Username: Rosyontravel
BIO: Travel and Instagram tips developer. I am Twin.
Working Mom
Contact: rtineva8o@gmail.com
Call to action: Tag photos with @rosyontravel to get
featured.

Chapter 6: Homework Tasks

What kind of product/service do you want to promote through Instagram?

....

....

Instagram Username

Write down twenty (20) keywords that come to your mind regarding your product/service?

....

....

Make combinations of all 20 keywords and try to create your USERNAME? (Consider only name easy to write/pronounce/understand).

....

....

Create your Instagram Username follow all tips in paragraph: **INSTAGRAM USERNAME.**

....

....

Instagram name

Think about keywords relevant to your niche to insert in your Name section.

....

....

Think about Emojis relevant to your brand and that adds value to your Name bio. Check how popular the emojis are?

....

....

Create (three) 3 different Name options, using only 30 characters. (Including emojis).

....

....

Create your Instagram Name, you can consult paragraph: **INSTAGRAM NAME.**

••

••

Instagram Bio

Create your Bio section, please consult paragraph: **INSTAGRAM BIO.**
Think about your Bio section (150 characters, excluded 30 characters of Name section). And create 3 different options of Bio. Use hashtags and keywords as well.

....

....

Instagram Clickable link

Create Clickable links, please consult paragraph: **INSTAGRAM CLICKABLE LINK.**
Think about what kind of product you can sell with your profile and where your followers can find this product into internet space?

....

....

Create links to insert in your bio.

....

....

Picture

Think about the picture that you want to use? The picture must be coherent with your brand profile.

....

Create a Profile Picture, consult paragraph: **INSTAGRAM PROFILE PICTURE**.

Conclusions

Congratulation that you finish, the second book of my Serial collection: Instagram Secrets. Remember that if you want to turn your profile visitors into followers you only have 150 characters in your description, one external link, and another 30 characters in your username in which to do this.

We learned that a Good Instagram Profile:

❖ Make it easy for followers to get in touch with you.

❖ Communicate essential information about your brand or unique selling point (USP).

❖ Present you, your personality, and your brand. It has to match the style and tone of voice you've emulated on your other social media platforms. It's no good if your Facebook page, for example, looks and reads entirely differently as this will be more likely to confuse your audience.

❖ Be a platform for sharing valuable information and have activities that your target audience can engage with like registering for an in-store event, brand testing, or clicking a link to your online store.

❖ Use SEO tactics in your Instagram bio username section to create opportunities to rank in search engine results. For example, instead of just adding your name or your brand name in that section of your bio, also add any relevant keywords.

Now you know something more about Instagram. I can define the Secrets of Instagram as 3C: Coherence, Constancy, and Competition. Think about these three inputs for your future Instagram strategy.

Other books

I hope that this book added value and quality to your social knowledge. If you enjoyed this book and found some benefit in reading this, I'd like to inform you that you can find in the Kindle store (Amazon) the following short guides that make part of the serial set.

Instagram Secrets Vol 1: HOW to find the right Instagram AUDIENCE. Become an influencer and build a business with no money on Instagram. (Short social media marketing book).

Instagram Secrets Vol 2: HOW to Build the Perfect Instagram Profile. Become an influencer and build a business with no money on Instagram. (Short social media marketing book).

Instagram Secrets Vol 3: HOW to CREATE Instagram KILLER CONTENTS. Become an influencer and build a business with no money on Instagram. (Short social media marketing book).

Instagram Secrets Vol 4 HOW to OUTSMART Instagram ALGORITHM. Become an influencer and build a business with no money on Instagram. (Short social media marketing book).

Instagram Secrets Vol 5: HOW to use Instagram HASHTAGS. Become an influencer and build a business with no money on Instagram. (Short social media marketing book).

Instagram Secrets Vol 6: HOW to use Instagram METRICS. Become an influencer and build a business with no money. (Short social media marketing book).

Instagram Secrets Vol 7: HOW to use Instagram DIRECT Messaging, Become an influencer and build a business with no money on Instagram. (Short social media marketing book).

Instagram Secrets Vol 8: HOW to use Instagram IGTV content. Become an influencer and build a business with no money on Instagram. (Short social media marketing book).

Instagram Secrets Vol 9: HOW to use Instagram CONTESTS. Become an influencer and build a business with no money on Instagram. (Short social media marketing book).

Instagram Secrets Vol 10: HOW to use Instagram INFLUENCERS. Become an influencer and build a business with no money on Instagram. (Short social media marketing book).

Instagram Secrets Vol 11: HOW to use Instagram AUTOMATION TOOLS. Become an influencer and build a business with no money on Instagram. (Short social media marketing book)

Instagram Secrets Vol 12: How to generate PROFITS from Instagram. Become an influencer and build a business with no money on Instagram. (Short social media marketing book).

Do not forget about my special Bonus. Get one of my books for free just sending me your email at rtineva80@gmail.com.

About the author

Rosy Toneva is a Marketing B2B and Commercial expert for some of the largest European Airlines. She enjoys traveling, writing, snapping pictures. She spends time daily writing her Instagram blog @rosyontravel. She believes in one religion - Traveling!

Rosy loves educating and inspiring other people to succeed and live the life of their dream. She always repeats: If more than 50% of your brain believes it, it will come true.

Rosy believe that social media allows people to interact with others and offer multiple ways for marketers to reach and engage with consumers.

Now the author would like to share with you how she started this project.

In April 2019, she decided to test her Instagram profile for professional use, instead of personal. She wanted to grow her Instagram through her two passions, "Travel and Marketing". At the time, @rosyontravel had around 560 followers. Rosy wanted to increase her followers in an organic way (no buying fake followers), no huge investing. She just desired to see what she could do by putting forth a conscious effort as a normal person did. It's been an intense four-month experiment of seeing what works and what doesn't. After only four months, she gained 10k loyal followers.

Thanks to her tests she prepared a set of twelve books, named Instagram secrets that you can find in Amazon. The advantage of these books is that they are very simple and do not offer trivial tips.

Follow Rosy Toneva Instagram profile (@rosyontravel) to get further information and updated news about Instagram.

If you want to know more about Instagram secrets methods described in this book, please contact Rosy Toneva personally to get her private lessons. Send an email to rtineva80@gmail.com or use Instagram Direct messaging.

One last thing

If you enjoyed this book and found some benefit in reading this, I'd like to hear from you and hope that you could take some time to post a review on Amazon. Your feedback and support will help me to greatly improve my writing craft for future projects and make this book even better.

Thank you and I wish you all the best in your future success

Common Instagram terms you should know

Bio - This is the biography of your profile on Instagram. This is your place to tell the world a little bit about yourself. You can use text, emojis, hashtags, and even '@' mention profiles here.

Mention - This is how you get someone's attention on Instagram. Begin with the @ symbol, followed by their handle or name. If you're following them, you'll find their handle in the first couple of autocomplete options. You can mention someone in a variety of places on Instagram, including in your bio, comments, or even in Instagram Stories.

Tag - Tag is different from Mention. You can only tag a person on a picture or a video. When you tag someone, it will show up in their profile (in the tagged section next to their Gallery).

Instagram Algorithm – An algorithm is a detailed step-by-step instruction set or formula for solving a problem or completing a task. In computing, programmers write algorithms that instruct the computer how to perform a task. Instagram Algorithm is several rules that the application follows to protect her community from spamming users and to set up the company earning a strategy.

Instagram Bots – These are automated profiles masquerading as people. But sometimes, even legit profiles use automated bots (third-party services) to get your attention. If you come across random comments on your posts or a slew of likes seconds after you post a picture, a bot was probably involved in the process.

Business Profile -   Instagram offers a simple way to switch from a personal profile to a business profile. You don't even need to be a registered business to use a business profile. And there are many advantages to converting to a business profile. You get access to action buttons in the bio and you get detailed insights from your followers. Plus, using a business profile is the only way to unlock features like embedding links in Stories and adding buy buttons to your posts.

Insights - Once you've converted to a Business Profile, you'll see an Insights button in the top toolbar in your profile. Tap on it and you'll find a sea of useful information. You'll find out what the age and gender breakdown of your followers is, as well as the best time to post to Instagram for maximum engagement.

Explore page - Tap on the Search button from the bottom toolbar and you'll end up in the Explore tab. This is the hodgepodge of everything that's trending on Instagram right now. On the top, you'll find topics, and below, a feed of popular photos and videos.

Home page - The Home screen is the list of activities of all the users you follow. Also referred to as the feed.

Swipe up –It is a feature that allows you to add links to your stories. Now, all Instagram business accounts with 10,000 or more followers can add links to Instagram Stories. Up until recently, this feature was only available to verified Instagram accounts (accounts with sign V).

IGTV - IGTV video is an app that can be used alone or in tandem with Instagram. It's essentially Instagram's answer to YouTube.

Instagram Stories - is a feature within the Instagram app where users can capture and post related images and video content in a slideshow format. In both apps, content is available for only 24 hours from the time of posting. Stories allow the addition of text, drawings, and emoticons to images or video clips.

Instagram contest - is a great way to get more followers, build an engaged audience and grow your brand. The contest is a promotional scheme in which participants compete for prizes by accomplishing something that requires skill. Although no fee is charged for participating in a contest.

API – The term API is an acronym, and it stands for "Application Programming Interface." The API is not the database or even the server, it is the code that governs the access point(s) for the server. They allow us to go get data from outside sources. To explain this better, let us take a familiar example. Imagine you're sitting at a table in a restaurant with a menu of choices to order from. The kitchen is part of the "system" that will prepare your order. What is missing is the critical link to communicate your order to the kitchen and deliver your food back to your table. That's where the waiter or API comes in. The waiter is the messenger – or API – that takes your request or order and tells the kitchen – the system – what to do. Then the waiter delivers the response back to you; in this case, it is the food.

IP Address - It's a network address for your computer so the Internet knows where to send you emails, data, and pictures.
With this short guide, I'm going to give you a deep dive into how to use Instagram hashtags to increase your followers. Using the right hashtags is fundamental. If you include the right Instagram hashtags on your posts or stories, you will likely see higher engagement than you would if you didn't have any.

Instagram organic follower growth - An organic follower growth rate means that an influencer attracts more followers over time with his or her content, gains more attention, and becomes more popular. The organic growth is based on genuine followers who are honestly interested in the content of the influencer shares.

Instagram Creator Studio - Instagram creator studio helps Instagram users to manage their Instagram presence much more conveniently. The Creator Studio was only available for Facebook pages earlier, is now available for Instagram business and creator accounts. Note that Creator Studio for both Instagram and Facebook is only available on desktop now. You can find inside Instagram Creator Studio the following information:
- Detailed growth data and Insights
- Number of daily activities
- Scheduling posts.
- Simplified messaging on Instagram since you have access to all the comments and messages all in one place.
- Use a set of cool soundtracks for Instagram videos for more impressions.

Instagram proxies - a proxy is a server that acts as an intermediary for its user's requests. In the beginning, proxy servers were used only for privacy and anonymity. Instagram proxies are developed to be used by marketers to automate several social media accounts at the same time. There are only a few proxy providers offering Instagram proxies because social networks are some of the most restrictive websites proxies. For Instagram, proxies are used to connect an Instagram account permanently through a single dedicated IP address in this way, one person can control several accounts. And vice-versa, one Instagram profile can be managed by several employees working remotely

VPN - Virtual Private Network, allows you to create a secure connection to another network over the Internet. People get VPNs for "privacy and security".

Are you confused between VPN and Proxies? VPN and proxies both help to keep users anonymous
VPN is almost similar to the Proxies, but its lot more versatile and most safe. Another best thing about VPN is that it encrypts 100% of your internet traffic and routes it through VPN servers making you entirely anonymous.

Printed in Great Britain
by Amazon

35170269R00040